THE TARDIGRADE

Do Your Kids Know This?

A Children's Picture Book
Amazing Creature Series

Tanya Turner

PUBLISHED BY:

Tanya Turner

Copyright © 2016

TABLE OF CONTENTS

The Tardigrade 5

Getting to Know Tardigrades 6

Where Can You Find Tardigrades? 9

How Do Tardigrades Behave? 11

What Do Tardigrades Eat? 15

How Do Tardigrades Breed and Reproduce? 17

What are the Predators of Tardigrades? 17

Tardigrades as Pets 19

Tardigrades and Humans 21

Say Hello to Tardigrades 21

The Tardigrade

The Tardigrade.
Image from Shutterstock by Sebastian Kaulitzki.

Heads up! You are about to meet a really cool animal called the Tardigrade.

Tardigrades are also called Water Bears and Moss Piglets. Let's find out why.

They live in the water and they are frequently found in the moss (which is also their food). They somewhat look like a pig, too – but since they're small (very, VERY small) they are called piglets instead of pigs.

Looking at it, you might also associate it with bears. It somewhat looks like a teddy bear. It even looks like a stuffed toy. If you get the opportunity to see it move, you will see that it somewhat walks like a bear as well.

Here's the ironic part. Tardigrades as very small creatures – in fact, they're microscopic (which means that you need a microscope to see them clearly), but bears and pigs are big creatures.

Believe it or not, Tardigrades are actually tougher than bears and pigs. If there was a matchup between Tardigrades, bears, and pigs – bet on the Tardigrades.

Here's some good news for you: you can keep a Tardigrade as a pet!

Tardigrades can be found all over the world. They could even be living somewhere close to you right now.

After reading this book, you will know how to find Tardigrades, how to catch them, and even how to take care of them!

Getting to Know Tardigrades

Tardigrades are microscopic creatures – they're very, VERY small. In fact, a full grown adult Tardigrade will only measure about 0.02 inch. That's so small that you won't be able to see this animal without a microscope. Maybe if you have really good eye sight, there's a chance that you will be able to see it – but you still won't be able to see it in detail.

Under the microscope, you will see that a Tardigrade is a strange-looking animal. Its body is made up of many segments, or parts (like spiders), and you will see the divisions clearly. In general, however, they are considered to be short, chubby organisms.

Tardigrades are small microorganisms. You need a microscope to see them.
Image from Shutterstock by royaltystockphoto.com.

Tardigrades have eight short (but thick) legs. The first pair of legs (those nearest the head) is used for holding on to things (such as food). The other three pairs of legs are used for walking.

The feet of Tardigrades have claws – but the numbers can differ. They can have anywhere from four to eight claws per foot.

It may be difficult to see the mouth of the Tardigrade – but they do have mouths. Their mouths look like tubes (because they use these to suck things, like food). They also have a sharp mouthpiece that they use for piercing – again, they prick objects or things when they need to eat (they can prick plants, cells, etc.).

Tardigrades have tube-like mouths.
Image from Shutterstock by royaltystockphoto.com.

Although they don't have respiratory organs (like lungs in people and gills in fish), they can still breathe. This species is designed in such a way that gas (or air) can travel throughout its whole body naturally.

Do Tardigrades have brains? Yes, they do – but are they capable of thinking? Well, that's something that hasn't been discovered yet.

Tardigrades live in moist environments.
Image from Shutterstock by royaltystockphoto.com.

Where Can You Find Tardigrades?

Tardigrades are found all over the world. They're literally everywhere (well, almost).

Tardigrades have been known to exist at the top of mountains, and they can also be found in the deep sea.

Tropical rainforests have Tardigrades living in them and they are also found in hot springs. In the Antarctic, they have been found living in layers of solid ice, and on the ocean floor, they can be found in the sand.

As you can see, Tardigrades exist in different environments and are used to extreme temperatures and conditions.

They can also live in mild (normal) environments. That's why you can also see them in ponds, lakes, meadows, and building walls. They're literally everywhere!

What they really need to exist is some kind of moisture (or water). For this reason, moss usually has Tardigrades because of its wet and moist nature.

A model of Tardigrade displayed in a museum.
Image from Flickr by Eden, Janine and Jim.

How Do Tardigrades Behave?

As water-dwelling microorganisms, Tardigrades consider water and anywhere with moisture their homes. Since they're living in a moist background, there's always an abundance of food everywhere because this can also be the breeding ground of bacteria (they eat bacteria).

As previously mentioned, Tardigrades are very tough. They're even tougher than bears and pigs. This microorganism can survive extreme conditions that would otherwise kill other animals (even the strongest of animals).

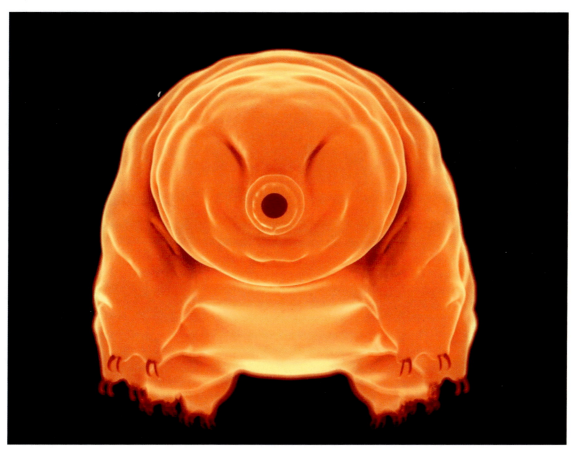

Tardigrades look like piglets – that's why they're called Moss Piglets.
Image from Shutterstock by Sebastian Kaulitzki.

When it comes to extreme temperatures, they can survive very hot and very cold temperatures. This means that they will remain alive even if exposed to fire (like in cooking) and ice (like snow).

They also hold up well in environments with very high pressure. If you didn't know it, deep oceans have very high pressure (that's why people can't go in very deep waters without proper gear). The Tardigrades, on the other hand, can withstand up to six times the pressure of the deepest oceans in the world.

Tardigrades have sharp mouthparts for piercing.
Image from Shutterstock by Giovanni Cancemi.

Tardigrades can even survive radiation. Radiation is very deadly – that's why people avoid being exposed to it. Humans can tolerate very small doses of radiation (such as when people have x-rays in hospitals). However, constant exposure to radiation is still dangerous because a person's body is not designed to withstand constant exposure to this element.

Tardigrades, on the other hand, can survive exposure to very high radiation. In short, they will still remain alive after being exposed to 100 times more than the lethal dosage of radiation for humans. In this particular case, we can say that Tardigrades are 100 times stronger than people when it comes to exposure to radiation.

Let's talk about the outer space for a while, shall we?

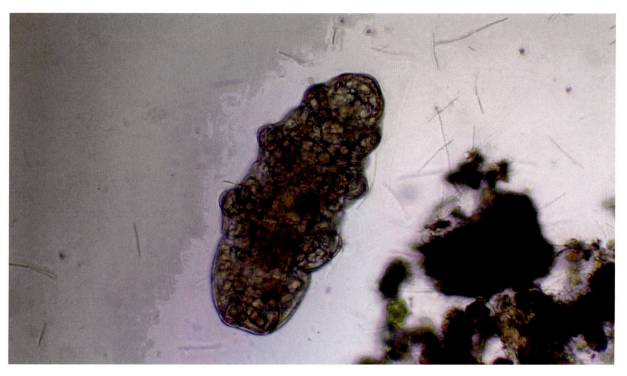

Tardigrades are very tough and can live through extreme conditions.
Image from Wikimedia by Dmitry Brant.

Outer space has a vacuum that (again) has very high pressure. That's the reason astronauts need to wear suits when they go into outer space. Tardigrades don't need space suits to survive in outer space because they can handle the atmosphere with no problem at all.

Just like every other living creature, Tardigrades also need food and water. However, they can live without food and water for many, many years. People will only last for a few days without eating or drinking anything, but Tardigrades can live for about 30 years without food and water. In this scenario, the microorganism will start to dry out until only a very small percentage of water is left in its body. Being as tough as it is, it can survive with only 1% to 3% water content in its body (a person would already become dehydrated and die in this condition).

A model of Tardigrade.
Image from Flickr by Katexic Clippings Newsletter.

Even their recovery system is very effective when they are deprived of food and water. Even after about 30 years, they will immediately rehydrate and recover when exposed to water and moisture again.

Can Tardigrades die (at all)? Actually, they can. As tough as they are, going for very long periods of exposure to unfavorable circumstances can kill them. It then becomes hard for them to remain alive for 100 years without food and water – because at this point, they will probably have 0% moisture in their bodies.

Tardigrades will only die if they are exposed to unfavorable conditions for a very long time.
Image from Shutterstock by Giovanni Cancemi.

What Do Tardigrades Eat?

Tardigrades are plant eaters, bacteria eaters, and meat eaters. Fortunately, plants, bacteria, and meat are always present in their immediate environment.

Since they are mostly found in moss, they can eat algae and the moss itself. Since a moist environment is a breeding ground for bacteria, they will also have bacteria on their menu frequently.

As meat eaters, you might think that they would find it hard to find meat sources in moss. Actually, the larvae form of crustaceans like crabs and shrimps start out so very small that they can be eaten by Tardigrades. Tardigrades are known to eat other Tardigrades.

Tardigrades can be found all over the world.
Image from Shutterstock by Sebastian Kaulitzki.

How Do Tardigrades Breed and Reproduce?

The reproductive organs of Tardigrades are located just above their intestines. When it's breeding season, a male and a female Tardigrade will mate. This is done during the molting season when the microorganism is also shedding its outer skin.

As oviparous creatures, Tardigrades give birth by laying eggs. It will take about 14 days for their eggs to hatch – and by then, young Tardigrades will come out of the eggs.

Since young Tardigrades already have adult cells in their bodies, they will quickly mature into adults. While developing and growing, the cells in their bodies will grow to make them bigger. This is a rather unusual development process since animals usually grow by cell division.

What are the Predators of Tardigrades?

Since they are microscopic animals, big animals like bears, pigs, lions, wolves, etc. are not really after Tardigrades. In their own little world (in moss), other microorganisms like amoebas can eat Tardigrades. Don't forget either that Tardigrades prey on other (smaller) Tardigrades, so they eat each other, so to speak.

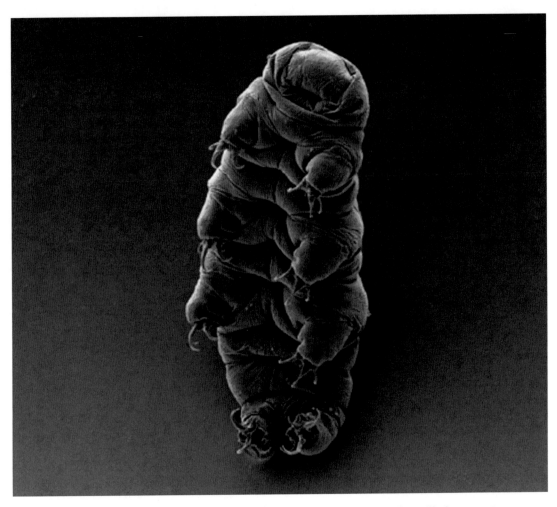

Tardigrades look like bears when they walk – that's why they're also called Water Bears.
Image from Wikimedia by Goldstein lab.

Finding Tardigrades is easy and they can be kept as pets.
Image from Shutterstock by royaltystockphoto.com.

Tardigrades as Pets

Tardigrades make interesting pets, and the good news is that you can easily find one (for free) and take care of it

Just follow the steps below.

1. Find some moss (you can look around in your backyard).
2. Place the moss in a shallow dish and put some water in it.
3. Let the moss soak in the water for about 8 to 24 hours.
4. Squeeze the water out of the moss into a container.

5. Take the container and place it under a microscope.

6. You will find one or more Tardigrades in the water. If not, repeat the process using another batch of moss. There's a good chance that you will be successful in your first attempt since they are in abundance everywhere.

7. If you find some Tardigrades, congratulations! Just place them in moss and make sure that the moss is always moist. You can now enjoy the company of your new pet.

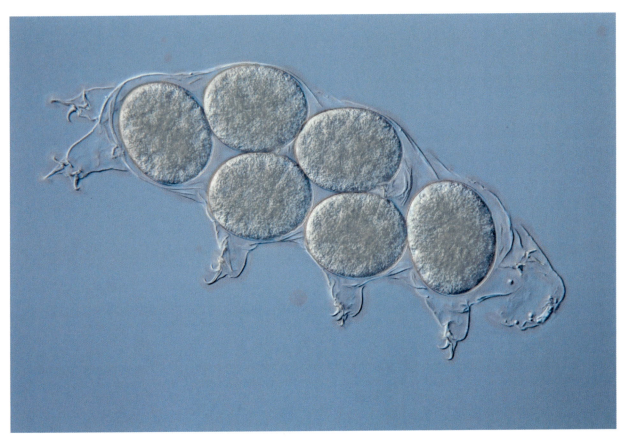

A Tardigrade with eggs inside its body.
Image from Shutterstock by Lebendkulturen.de.

Tardigrades and Humans

Children, students, and young scientists will enjoy viewing and taking care of Tardigrades. Needless to say, they are very interesting creatures – and it would be fun to monitor their movements and activities throughout the day.

They are easy to find since they are basically everywhere. They are also easy to take care of and very hard to kill.

With other pets, you need to worry about building them homes and cages. This is not so with the Tardigrades because a shallow dish can be their entire universe.

People need a microscope to fully enjoy viewing a Tardigrade though. They can be seen by a low-powered microscope (an inexpensive microscope), so there is no need to get a high-powered, expensive one. They can actually be seen with the naked eye, but viewing them under a microscope is the best option because you will be able to see all their movements as if it were a big animal.

Say Hello to Tardigrades

Tardigrades are related to spiders, crustaceans, and insects. As you can already tell, however, they are more impressive than their distant relatives. Their survival abilities make all other living creatures seem weak – including humans.

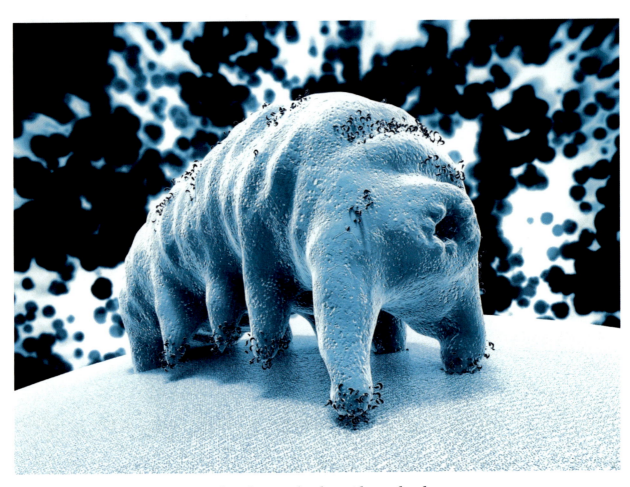

Tardigrades are related to spiders and crabs.
Image from Shutterstock by royaltystockphoto.com.

The Tardigrade is an amazing animal.
Image from Shutterstock by Sebastian Kaulitzki.

So, what are you waiting for? Try to find a Tardigrade soon and enjoy its company in a saucer.

Disclaimer

The information contained in this book is for general information purposes only. The information is provided by the authors and, while we endeavor to keep the information up to date and correct, we make no representations or warranties of any kind, expressed or implied, about the completeness, accuracy, reliability, suitability or availability with respect to the book or the information, products, services, or related graphics contained in the book for any purpose. Any reliance you place on such information is therefore strictly at your own risk.

Made in the USA
Columbia, SC
11 January 2021